PEOPLE IN COSTUME

The 1950s and 1960s

JENNIFER RUBY

1962

1950

B.T. Batsford . London

ACKNOWLEDGEMENTS

With love and thanks to my dear friends Monica, Marie, Rose and Lew and to my parents, who all shared their memories of the 1950s.

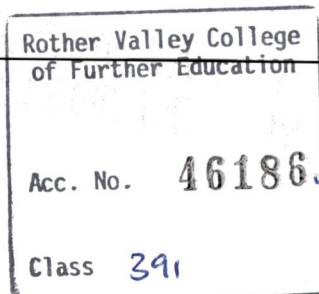

© Jennifer Ruby 1994
First Published 1994

Typeset and print in Hong Kong
by World Print Ltd.
for the Publishers
B.T. Batsford Ltd
4 Fitzhardinge Street
London W1H 0AH

A CIP catalogue record for this book is available from the British Library.

ISBN 0 7134 7217 0

CONTENTS

Look at the two girls on this page. One of them is dressed in the fashion of 1959, the other in the fashion of 1989. Can you tell which is which?

INTRODUCTION

The 1950s and 1960s were years of great change when almost anything anything seemed possible. In 1950 Britain was still recovering from World War II and food and clothes rationing were still in force. Gradually, however, restrictions were lifted. People began to feel more relaxed and light-hearted and started spending money on lots of exciting new products that were around.

Advances in science meant new labour-saving devices for the home. More cars were bought and people travelled more widely. Fashionable clothes were being mass-produced which made them cheaper and meant that greater numbers of people could afford to buy them.

For the first time in history, young people began to influence pop music, fashion and ideas. Thousands of teenagers copied the styles of groups like The Beatles and The Rolling Stones and young, energetic designers like Mary Quant and John Stephen revolutionised the fashion industry with their colourful and exciting designs.

Let us now imagine that we are in the early 1950s and meet Alan, who is a Teddy Boy.

THE CORONATION, 1953

"My friends are I are called Teddy Boys because of the style of clothes that we wear. It is very smart and consists of a long jacket, tight, drainpipe trousers, bright socks, (my favourite ones are yellow), and creepers, which are large, crepe-soled shoes like boats. We also like to wear brass rings called knuckledusters and thin, bootlace ties. We have a particular hairstyle too which we like to keep just so. It is slicked back from the forehead and brushed to a point at the back and the style is kept in place with cream. You can see me at the hairdressers in the picture below having my hair dressed in the Teddy Boy style.

Now I am going to take you on a journey through the 1950s and 1960s and introduce you to several different characters from that time so that you can see the kind of clothes that they wore and imagine the kind of lives they led."

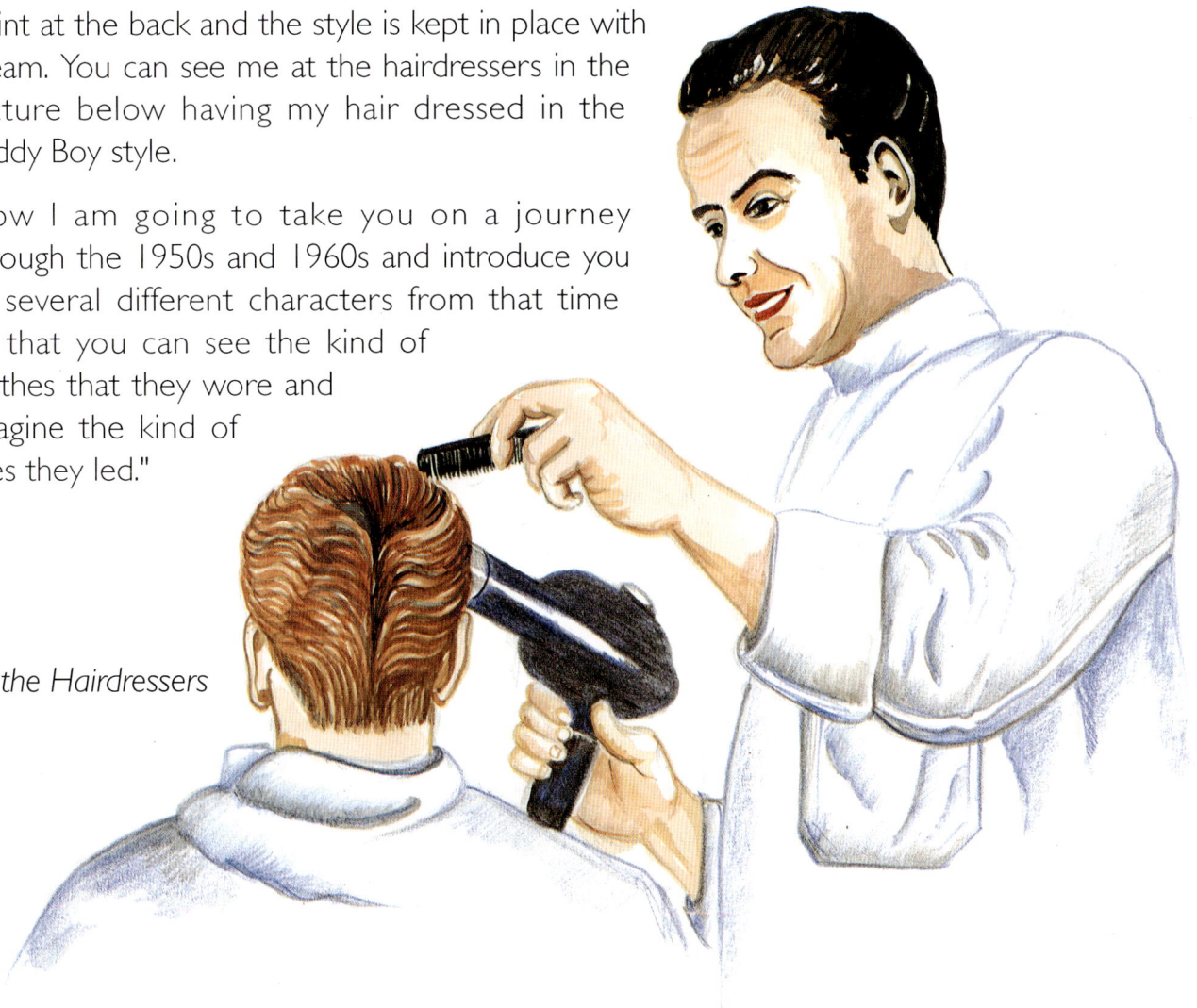

At the Hairdressers

LADIES' FASHIONS

It is June 1953 and whole country is in a fever of excitement as the new Queen Elizabeth is to be crowned in Westminster Abbey. All kinds of celebrations are being planned from tea parties to banquets.

Geraldine, Alice and Cynthia are sisters. They live in London. They are going to the coronation and will be attending a banquet in the evening.

Geraldine is wearing a gold and black rayon dress with a black hat and shoes. Her sister Alice has on a black and white checked suit with astrakhan cuffs and Cynthia is wearing a full-skirted coat with a belt in the middle. Both ladies have small neat hats to match their outfits.

Geraldine

Cynthia

Alice

EVENING WEAR

On these two pages you can see the sort of clothes that will be worn to the evening banquet. Robert is Geraldine's husband. He is wearing a suit of midnight blue with black braid down the trouser leg. His suit is deep blue rather than black as black tends to look greenish in artificial light at night. He also has on a silk bow tie, a pleated white shirt and black shoes. Round his middle he is wearing a cummerbund which is a kind of wide sash. It is pleated and worn with the pleats pointing upwards so that if he were going to the theatre or the opera he could keep his tickets in there!

On the right Geraldine and Alice are pictured in their evening gowns. They are very beautiful and luxurious with lots of material in the full skirts. Geraldine and Alice find these styles lovely to wear after the skimpy clothes that they had to wear during the war-years when material was in short supply.

Robert

Geraldine

Alice

CLOTHES FOR A GARDEN PARTY

Monica, Rose and Lewis are friends and live just outside London. They are going to a garden party to celebrate the coronation.

Monica is wearing a two-piece outfit of maroon satin, with black shoes and black lace gloves. Monica has very cleverly made her hat herself from a bicycle wheel which she covered with black lace and ribbon.

Rose is wearing a cream coloured suit of light-weight woollen material with a sleeveless floral print blouse. She has pearls at her neck and small neat earrings. Lewis has on a grey suit with a white shirt and dark tie.

Can you draw pictures of some of the other guests?

Monica

Rose

Lewis

PREPARING FOR A STREET PARTY

This is Lewis's brother Joe. He lives in a small town with his wife Carol and their two young children. The whole family is going to watch the coronation on a neighbour's television set, then they will join in a street party to celebrate.

Joe is wearing a white cotton shirt with the sleeves rolled up, blue baggy trousers and a brown leather belt.

You can see Carol and her sister Ivy on the opposite page. Carol is a good cook and she has been busy making cakes for the street party. She has on a green cotton dress, a floral apron and has her hair in a turban.

Ivy is wearing a lilac coloured twin set and a pleated skirt. She has pearls at her neck and a matching bracelet.

Can you draw a picture of the street party?

Joe

Carol

Ivy

AT THE SEASIDE, 1958

During the 1950s many more people bought cars and motor scooters were popular with young people. This meant that people travelled about more on day trips and family holidays. Let us now move forward to 1958 and imagine that we are at a seaside resort.

Here is Lewis, who has brought Rose to the coast for the day. He is wearing a sports jacket, an open-necked shirt, trousers with turn-ups and lace-up shoes.

Rose is wearing a brightly coloured skirt with an elasticated waist and matching bra top. Over this she has on a light jacket. She is also wearing open toed sandals and matching necklace, bracelet and earrings.

You can also see two teenagers in the picture. Margaret (in the background), is wearing cropped cotton trousers, a halter-neck sun top, a wide black belt and sunglasses.

Jennifer is on her motor scooter. She has on trousers, a light jacket and a floral headscarf. She is going to meet a friend and spend the day with her so she has brought some other clothes with her in the basket on the back of her scooter.

Lewis

Margaret

Jennifer

Rose

254 TJR.

TJR

A FAMILY OUTING

Here are Monica, her husband John and their small daughter Vivienne who have come to the coast for the day to visit their relations.

John is wearing a yellow and blue sweater that Monica knitted for him, a white shirt, a blue spotted cravat, beige trousers and lace-up shoes.

Monica is a good needlewoman and has made her own and Vivienne's outfits. Monica has on a yellow and red cotton dress and white leather sandals. Vivienne is wearing a cotton dress in lilac and white with smocking on the bodice, a white cardigan and white socks and shoes.

YOUNG FASHION

Jennifer has now met up with her friend Jane. They have been walking along the promenade and sitting on the beach.

On this page Jane is wearing a brightly coloured sundress that has a matching short-sleeved jacket.

Jane

Jennifer has changed from her scooter gear into Italian-style pedal pushers, a sleeveless top, a cotton jacket and flat shoes. She has pinned her long hair up under a sombrero. You can also see Jane in her bathing costume.

In the evening the girls will go dancing at the Mecca. Their favourite star is Elvis Presley, who you can see on the next page.

Jane

Jennifer

AT THE MECCA

Here is Jennifer dancing to the music of Elvis Presley. She is wearing a yellow blouse with cap sleeves, a flared cotton skirt over a white petticoat, and black high-heeled shoes. Her partner is wearing a blue wool sweater, a white shirt, straight trousers and brown suede shoes.

Do you know what kind of dance they are doing?

GOING TO A RESTAURANT

John

Monica

Monica and John are also going out for the evening. They are going to a restaurant with Monica's cousin Peggy.

John is wearing a single breasted, three-piece suit, a trilby hat and leather gloves. Monica has on a wool suit and a hat that she has knitted herself. It is called a 'Jellybag hat'. She has pearls around her neck and a black handbag and shoes.

Peggy is wearing a duster coat. This is a loose, flared, unlined summer coat that is nice and light for the summer evening.

Peggy

CARNABY STREET, 1966

Now we will move forward to the year 1966 and visit Carnaby Street in London. This street is very famous as a fashion centre and is full of boutiques that sell colourful and exciting clothes.

This is John Stephen who owns a boutique in Carnaby Street. Like Mary Quant, he is completely changing the clothing market with his new ideas. He is a very quiet man and likes to dress conventionally himself but his shop sells outrageously bright men's clothes in unusual fabrics.

On the far right you can see two customers at John's boutique. The man on the left is wearing a pink velvet jacket, a floral shirt and matching kipper tie, corduroy trousers and a leather belt and suede shoes. His friend is wearing a Union Jack jacket and blue jeans.

The following lines were sung by the pop group The Kinks in 1966:

"They seek him here, they seek him there,
His clothes are loud, but never square....
He's a dedicated follower of fashion."

Can you find out more about men's clothes in the 1960s?

THE MINI SKIRT

Mary Quant was the designer who made the mini skirt popular and Twiggy, the model pictured below, was the ideal shape to wear it as she was so slim. With her long legs, short hair and huge eyes rimmed with black mascara, she presented a 'boyish' look that thousands of women and young girls wanted to copy.

In the picture Twiggy is wearing a striped mini dress and low-heeled shoes. On the opposite page you can see some designs by Mary Quant from the 1960s.

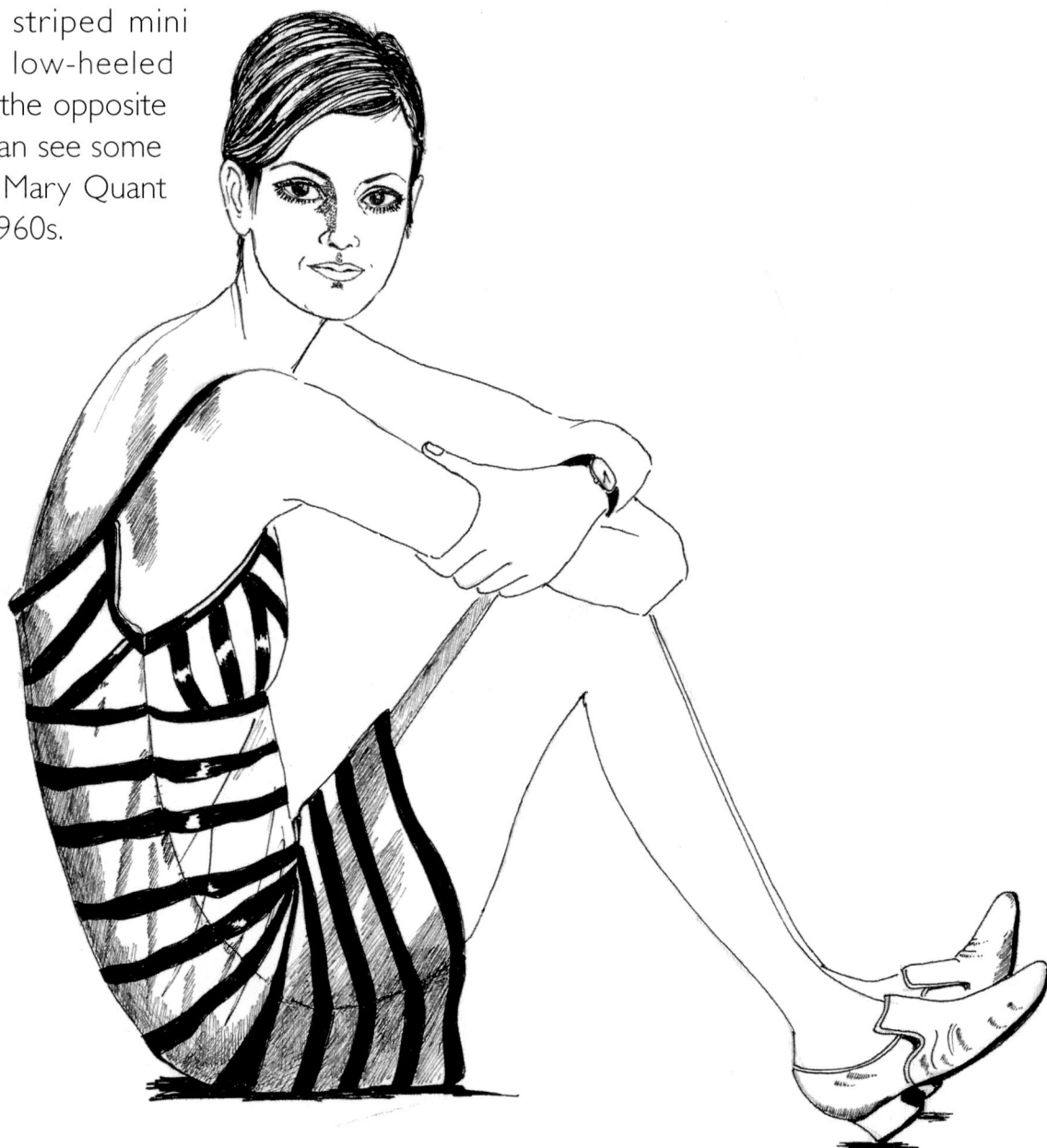

Knitted dress
and tights by
Mary Quant

Suit by
Mary
Quant

Handbag

Cotton blouse,
skirt with
braces

Matching underwear
and socks

THE ROMANTIC LOOK

In contrast to the simple shapes of the minis that you have just seen, a more romantic, frilly look was more popular in the mid 1960s, which is modelled here by Jennifer and her friend Jane.

Jennifer is wearing a cotton lace-edged blouse and bloomers and has her hair curled.

The pop singer Sandie Shaw won the Eurovision Song Contest in 1967 with the song 'Puppet on a String'. She appeared on stage wearing an outfit similar to Jennifer's and won the hearts of the voters!

Jennifer

Jane is wearing a cotton nightdress edged with frills.

See if you can find pictures of some of the famous models of the 1960s (for example, Jean Shrimpton, Patti Boyd and Twiggy), and draw pictures of the clothes they are wearing.

Jane

HOUSEWIVES' CHOICE

It is important to remember that not everyone wore the exaggerated fashions that were popular with the young. Many people preferred more conventional clothes.

Monica is busy cooking lunch for her friends Marjorie and Catherine who are coming to visit. She is wearing a woollen dress that has buttons to the waist and a flared skirt. Over this she has on a pretty apron. She is also wearing a pearl necklace and black, high-heeled shoes.

Monica

Marjorie is wearing a checked suit, matching hat, gloves and bag and black high-heeled shoes. Catherine is wearing a smart, light-weight raincoat with a matching hat, black gloves and shoes. She has a pretty floral scarf tucked around her neck.

Marjorie

Catherine

THE LONDON UNDERGROUND, 1968

The Queen opened the Victoria Line on the London Underground in 1968. Here you can see her taking a ride after the ceremony. This must have been an unusual experience for her! She is wearing a fur coat over a blue dress with a matching blue hat.

Over the next few pages you will meet various people who might use the underground for travel.

Gillian and Mark are hippies. They like to wear brightly coloured clothes, scarves and beads and often get ideas for their outfits by looking at the clothes worn by people in other countries. For example, they might wear Indian silks, or Moroccan robes and kaftans.

Here you can see them returning from a pop concert. They are wearing brightly coloured outfits and have painted their faces.

SNAPPY DRESSERS

Karen, Mike and Sarah all work in London and like to dress in the latest fashions.

Karen is wearing a yellow canvas coat, with black patches on the sleeves and pockets and a yellow hat. Under her coat she has on a short blue pleated skirt and blue jumper. Her boots come up to her thighs and are made of PVC.

Mike is wearing a three-piece suit with a colourful shirt and tie, short boots and a silver bracelet. Sarah has on a very short black and white coat and calf-length canvas boots with peep toes.

Karen

Mike

Sarah

THE INFLUENCE OF OTHER COUNTRIES

More people from foreign countries came to live in England during the 1960s and English people began to travel abroad more. This meant that fashions from far away places began to influence popular styles.

Lucy and Alma are friends who work in a London boutique. Lucy is wearing a fur hat, a knitted cardigan coat, jeans and suede boots. Can you guess which country influenced her outfit?

Alma has her hair tightly braided into long strips. This is called 'corn-sewing' the hair.

Janine works in a London shop that sells products from India. Her outfit is made from beautiful Indian silks.

Can you think of more ideas that have come from other countries?

Lucy

Alma

Janine

BELL-BOTTOM TROUSERS

Bell-bottom trousers were very popular in the 1960s. They were fitted to the knees and then flared out into very wide hems. Everyone loved them. There was even a pop song by Louden Wainwright devoted to them. It was called 'Bell-Bottom Pants' *

"Everybody's got the bell-bottom pants
Ain't got the pants you ain't got a chance
At the pop festival, rock festival, folk festival or the dance
Oh baby, them bell-bottom pants."

Dave, Christine and Sue are all wearing bell-bottom trousers. Dave has on a leather jacket, a silk shirt and bow tie and corduroy trousers. Christine has on a three-piece trouser suit and a kipper tie. Her hair is styled in flick-ups.

Sue has made her colourful trousers herself from a satin material. Over these she has on a three-quarter length jacket. She is carrying a leather shoulder bag.

Now we have finished our journey through the 1950s and 1960s and you have met several characters and have seen their different outfits. Over the next few pages you can see some other interesting features of the period.

Dave

* 'Pants' is the American word for trousers.

Sue

Christine

CHILDREN'S CLOTHES

On these two pages you can see examples of children's clothes of the 1950s and 1960s. They were simple in design and came in colourful materials that were easy to care for.

Quite a lot of children belonged to the Tufty Club. Can you find out what this was?

1952

1968

1959

1957

1959

1959

1969

The Tufty Club

HATS AND HAIRSTYLES

Women began to visit the hairdresser more often in the 1950s and 1960s. Some popular hairstyles are shown here. Mr. Teasy-Weasy and Vidal Sassoon were famous hairdressers of the time. Can you find out more about them?

the gamine look, 1956

a style created by Mr. Teasy-Weasy, late 1950s

1957

mid - 1950s

1955

hair backcombed into a beehive shape and combined with "flick-ups", 1961

the "five-point cut", a famous hairstyle created by Vidal Sassoon. 1964

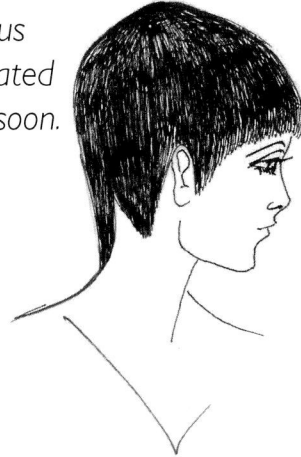

1963 - the classic "bob" that made Vidal Sassoon famous.

1965

1961

1963

ACCESSORIES

Here are some accessories from the 1950s and 1960s. Can you look at the date beside each one and decide which character in the book they might have belonged to?

Evening shawl and gloves, 1951

leather shoe, 1956

black and white plastic boot, 1962

satin evening bag, 1960

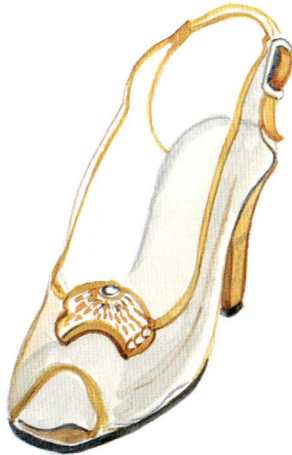

plastic shoes,
1955

sunglasses, 1954

black leather Beatle
boot, 1964

side-lace shoe in
brown leather,
1965

"bucket-type" handbag,
1955

red leather shoe with
black straps, 1962

plastic Scottie
dog brooch,
1956

THE INFLUENCE OF POP MUSIC

Pop music had a very important influence on fashion in the 1950s and 1960s. Stars like Elvis Presley and Buddy Holly in the 1950s and groups like The Beatles and The Rolling Stones in the 1960s were adored by thousands of fans who listened to the words of their songs and copied the clothes they wore.

Here are some famous stars of the 1960s. On page 20 you saw Elvis Presley as he was in the 1950s. Can you find out more about the link between pop music and fashion? Do you think pop stars still influence fashion today?

The Beatles, in their Pierre Cardin "Beatle jackets" - c. 1962

Jimi Hendrix - who wore bright fabrics, clashing colours and jewellery.

Mick Jagger - who wore a white mini dress in Hyde Park

INDEX AND GLOSSARY